TED SHUTTLESWORTH

MINISTERING TO THOSE

OPPRESSED

OF THE DEVIL

Unless otherwise indicated, all Scripture quotations are from the King James Version of the Bible.

Ministering to Those Oppressed of the Devil
ISBN 978-1-7336042-6-0

www.tedshuttlesworth.com

Published by T.S.E.A., Inc.
Post Office Box 7
Farmington, West Virginia 26571
USA

Cover design by Ted Shuttlesworth Jr.

Printed in the United States of America

CONTENTS

INTRODUCTION

Every time that I walk out onto the platform, my eyes are immediately drawn to the souls that are in front of me. Whether it is thousands or hundreds, they have gathered to receive supernatural help from the Lord. The needs are many as some are dealing with cancer and others with nervous disorders. There are those who are battling fear and worry and are afflicted in mind and body . . . sick and diseased, bound by sin's power they are waiting for their deliverance.

My spirit is yielded to the Holy Spirit. Usually, I have spent the day studying the Word of God and praying. There are times the Lord leads me to fast for the meetings as well. God's work is serious business. It requires His ministers to be fully dedicated to the work of the ministry.

The songs of deliverance rise up to the Lord. The atmosphere is bathed in His presence. The wonderful Gifts of the Spirit begin to operate. Suddenly, there may be a message in other tongues which cuts through oppression. Perhaps the gift of prophecy brings comfort to these precious souls. There is a charging up by the Spirit, and the people feel it!

Jesus is here! All things are possible . . . ONLY BELIEVE. I have experienced the operation of the word of knowledge or discerning of spirits at these moments. The revelation gifts bring the manifestation of the working of miracles and the gifts of healing.

Oppression melts away, and joy fills and lifts the hearts!

It is time to minister to the oppressed and needy. You, too, can be used to minister to the oppressed if you will pay the price and commit yourself fully to the cause of Christ.

When the Lord turned again the captivity of Zion, we were like them that dream. Then was our mouth filled with laughter, and our tongue with singing: then said they among the heathen, The Lord hath done great things for them. The Lord hath done great things for us; whereof we are glad.

Psalm 126:1-3

Ted Shuttlesworth
Hill Cottage, January 2022

CHAPTER ONE

THE SOUND OF DELIVERANCE

The Spirit of the Lord is upon me, because he hath anointed me to preach the gospel to the poor; he hath sent me to heal the brokenhearted, to preach DELIVERANCE TO THE CAPTIVES, and recovering of sight to the blind, to set at liberty them that are bruised,

Luke 4:18

Jesus understood that mankind needed to be set free. He acknowledged that it took the anointing of the Holy Spirit to accomplish this task. He came into the temple in Nazareth, took the book of Isaiah, and read from chapter 61. Jesus knew that those who were oppressed and bound by the devil needed healing and deliverance. He told those that were gathered there, *"This day is this scripture fulfilled in your ears." (Luke 4:21)*

Isaiah prophesied to Israel concerning the problem that they were dealing with as a nation.

The captive exile hasteneth that he may be loosed, and that he should not die in the pit, nor that his bread should fail.

Isaiah 51:14

The captives were not only captives, but they were exiled. They were removed from where they were supposed to be. They were in a hurry to be loosed. When you are captive in any area of your life, your desire is to be free.

Satan tries to bind people, captivate them, and take them from their rightful place. The Lord God has come from Heaven and said, *"Enough is enough."* The captive is going to be loosed. You shall not die in the pit. He is *"not willing that any should perish, but that all should come to repentance."* (2 Peter 3:9)

What Isaiah prophesied as the problem in the 51st chapter, the Lord gave him the *solution* in the 61st chapter. It is the anointing of the Holy Spirit that came upon Jesus in the wilderness that sets the captive free.

But I am the Lord thy God that divided the sea, whose waves roared: the Lord of hosts is his name.

Isaiah 51:15

That's His Name! He's the Lord of Hosts!

We need to learn how to minister to those who are oppressed of the devil. This is the greatest challenge. God has a prescribed method to set men and women free that have been held captive and are exiled.

O bless our God, ye people, and make the voice of his praise to be heard:

Psalm 66:8

ANOINTED MUSIC DRIVES THE DEVIL OUT!

David knew how to praise God.

But the Spirit of the Lord departed from Saul, and an evil spirit from the Lord troubled him.

1 Samuel 16:14

This spirit that was allowed by God came and troubled him. When you are ministering to people that are oppressed of the devil, they have got trouble.

Trouble is in their minds.

Trouble is in their bodies.

Trouble is in their homes.

Trouble is in their checkbooks.

Trouble! We used to sing a song when I was younger, "Troubles in this Land will Soon be Over." Do you believe that?

Saul was lifted up in pride. He sent for a minstrel, David. *"And it came to pass, when the EVIL SPIRIT from God was upon Saul, that David took an harp, and PLAYED with his hand: so Saul was REFRESHED, and was WELL, and THE EVIL*

SPIRIT DEPARTED from him." (1 Samuel 16:24)

The King James records *"from God"* or allowed by God. God allows what you allow. You want to play with the devil? He will be there. Don't blame God for it. You want to stay sick and deny Christ's healing power? Don't blame God for your sickness or your disease. We are instructed to *"Study to shew thyself approved unto God, a workman that needeth not to be ashamed, rightly dividing the word of truth." (2 Timothy 2:15)* God is for you and not against you.

James wrote, *"Every good gift and every perfect gift is from above, and cometh down from the Father of lights," (James 1:17)* Sickness is not good. Trouble is not good. Sometimes we tie God's hands.

If God had sent the evil spirit to Saul, He would not have let David set Saul free from it. He would not let a natural man (David) go against His will if He were doing it.

Music has improved over the years from when David first played a harp. The instruments are better. The sound that amplifies the music is better.

ANOINTED MUSIC REFRESHES THE SOUL

One time, we were in meetings in the Albany, New York area. When the music started playing, a young Jewish woman on crutches that could not walk came for prayer. One leg had been crippled for some time. Her friend invited her to this Holy Ghost revival.

Holy Ghost revival is for the Jew, it is for the Greek, and

it is for everybody. The Apostle Paul reminds us, *"For I am not ashamed of the gospel of Christ: for it is the power of God unto salvation to everyone that believeth; to the Jew first, and also to the Greek."* (Romans 1:16)

When they started playing on the instruments, she threw her crutches up in the air; it looked like a winged-back car. She took off and ran across the front of the auditorium. Although she was not saved, there was something in that music that made the spirit of infirmity depart from her leg.

That is what happened when David played on the harp. The devil could not stay, and Saul was well and refreshed. I believe that there is coming a time in these meetings when the anointing gets in the music and praise that every one of you will leave well and refreshed.

Make a joyful noise unto the Lord, all ye lands. Serve the Lord with gladness: come before his presence with singing. Know ye that the Lord he is God: it is he that hath made us, and not we ourselves; we are his people, and the sheep of his pasture. Enter into his gates with thanksgiving, and into his courts with praise: be thankful unto him, and bless his name. For the Lord is good; his mercy is everlasting; and his truth endureth to all generations.

Psalm 100

Start getting happy and begin to praise the Lord. Sing a new song unto the Lord. Serve the Lord with gladness, not sadness. In some churches, people act like they were baptized in lemon juice; but as for me and my house, we are going to serve the Lord!

PRAISE SETS THE CAPTIVE FREE

When you come together, you come in thanking Him, and then you praise Him. Thanksgiving and praise are two forms of worship in your Bible. You start by thanking Him. Some churches have become like funeral homes. They play slow, dead, dry music. I have been in some places where I looked to see if a casket was coming down the aisle. I did not know that you could strum a guitar that slow. They had no joy and no victory. When you are ministering to the oppressed, do not add to their burdens with dry ecclesiastical-styled music.

The word for *"praise"* in your Bible is the word *"entheos."* Do you know what it means? It means *"fleshly demonstrations of joy."* Some may think, *"You should not act that way in church."* Fortunately, God does not think that way.

> **Praise ye the Lord Praise ye the name of the Lord praise him, O ye servants of the Lord. Ye that stand in the house of the Lord, in the courts of the house of our God,**
>
> **Psalm 135:1, 2**

ONE NIGHT IN THE TEMPLE

There was a woman in my wife's home church, Zion Gospel Temple, who had polio. One of her legs had a brace on her thigh and a hinge around the knee. The brace went down into her shoe. It was a Sunday night. The glory of God filled that auditorium. The people were praising the Lord. When suddenly, the power of God came on her. She was short and thin, and I saw her start to move. She lifted her hands, tears flowing down her cheeks and she let out a shout.

I had helped her go up the steps into the church that night. When the anointing hit her, she no longer needed help. She took off running. When she got down to the front altar, she began to dance before the Lord.

Something came loose in the upper part of the brace, and it loosened around her knee. She kicked her shoe off and ran around the church. She stood and moved her legs. What will your praise do? It will give you something from God that the devil cannot steal.

Praise is fleshly demonstrations of joy. Enthusiasm comes from the word *"entheos."*

Clap your hands. (Psalm 47:1)

Shout unto God. (Psalm 47:1)

Dance before the Lord. (Psalm 149:3)

Play skillfully with a loud noise. (Psalm 33:3)

How God ANOINTED Jesus of Nazareth with the Holy Ghost and with power: who went about doing

good, and healing all that were OPPRESSED of the devil; for God was with him.

Acts 10:38

There are certain things we can do to create this atmosphere for those who are bound. Isaiah touched on this when he prophesied, *"Therefore the redeemed of the Lord shall return, and come with singing unto Zion; and everlasting joy shall be upon their head: they shall obtain gladness and joy; and sorrow and mourning shall flee away." (Isaiah 51:11)*

We used to sing this verse as a song when we were in Bible School. The Lord has promised that sorrow and mourning (depression) would be replaced with singing, gladness, and joy. Hallelujah!

RELEASING JOY TO THE OPPRESSED

I read where an entire city was filled with joy after Philip, the evangelist, preached the delivering message of Jesus Christ to the people who were bound by spirits.

Then Philip went down to the city of Samaria, and PREACHED CHRIST unto them. And the people with one accord gave heed unto those things which Philip spake, HEARING AND SEEING THE MIRACLES which he did. For UNCLEAN SPIRITS, crying with loud voice, CAME OUT of many that were possessed with them: and many taken with palsies, and

that were lame, were healed. And there was GREAT
JOY in that city.

Acts 8:5-8

The message is Jesus! His message is different from
what the world is talking about. Simon, the sorcerer, heard
this deliverance message. He had been working witchcraft
over the people.

The word *"sorceries"* in *Acts 8:11* is the same word found
in *Revelation 9:21*. It is the Greek word *"pharmakia"* from
which we get our word *"pharmacy."* This is a spirit designed
in hell. People take pills to go to sleep and pills to wake up.
Drugs that cannot help because they are oppressed.

Simon, the sorcerer, the witchcraft worker, could not
keep the power of God from setting the people free! Whole
cities are going to be set free in the last days. Great joy is
going to fill the cities and the nations. Oppression will go,
and the joy of the Lord will come.

CHAPTER TWO

PREACHING DELIVERANCE TO THE OPPRESSED

The Spirit of the Lord is upon me, because he hath anointed me to PREACH the gospel to the poor; he hath sent me to heal the brokenhearted, to PREACH deliverance to the captives, and recovering of sight to the blind, to set at liberty them that are bruised.

Luke 4:18

The power to deliver people who are oppressed is released by the ministry of the Word of God. *"So then faith cometh by hearing, and hearing by the word of God."* (Romans 10:17) You, as a believer, can help turn the tide in your life and in the lives of others.

Jesus released the anointing by preaching, and then God would bring to pass the desired results for those who needed help and healing. We must give the Lord free reign to do what He wants to do. The Bible teaches us, *"But the word of God is not bound."* (2 Timothy 2:9)

If the Word is not bound, why then are people bound?

Many are bound by sickness, disease, afflictions, mental problems, and depression. Jesus gave us this example of ministry to bring healing to the people.

And Jesus went about all the cities and villages, TEACHING in their synagogues, and PREACHING the gospel of the kingdom, and HEALING EVERY SICKNESS AND EVERY DISEASE among the people.
Matthew 9:35

Here is the pattern of ministry that Jesus used to minister to the oppressed. He came teaching, preaching, and healing. Teaching is when you explain the Word. Preaching is when you proclaim the Word. The result is that healing comes in response to the Word.

The Lord promised the same results would happen for His disciples. *"And they went forth, and PREACHED everywhere, the Lord working with them, and confirming the word with signs following. Amen." (Mark 16:20)*

I SAW JESUS ONE NIGHT IN DALLAS

My wife, Bonnie, and I were sitting on the front row in an Evangelists Conference in Dallas, Texas. A great missionary evangelist, T. L. Osborn, was preaching. He said to us young folks, *"Give me your attention! You have got to keep the Gospel simple."*

He turned to a man seated in a wheelchair. His oppression was that he could not walk. He was not possessed, but oppressed by this affliction. Osborn told us that you don't ignore the need but he said, *"I would say to this man who is in this wheelchair, Jesus heals crippled people, He ministers to those who are oppressed."* Then Brother Osborn quoted this passage of Scripture:

> **And he was teaching in one of the synagogues on the Sabbath. And, behold, there was a woman which had a spirit of infirmity eighteen years, and was bowed together, and could in no wise lift up herself. And when Jesus saw her, he called her to him, and SAID unto her, WOMAN, THOU ART LOOSED FROM THINE INFIRMITY. And he laid his hands on her: and immediately she was made straight, and glorified God.**
>
> **Luke 13:10-13**

God's Word contains your miracle. It can drive out sickness, disease, affliction, heal sugar diabetes, heart trouble, cause the deaf to hear, and the blind to see.

God is setting people free in our meetings and we are seeing these miracles. Deaf ears are opening. People are healed in their bones and joints. God is setting them free. Why? His Word contains power. *"That power belongeth unto God."* *(Psalm 62:11)*

I have heard full-gospel ministers say, *"Don't seek what is in God's hands, but rather, seek God instead."* However, God Himself declared:

Thus saith the Lord, the Holy One of Israel, and his Maker, Ask me of things to come concerning my sons, and concerning the work of my hands COMMAND YE ME.

Isaiah 45:11

These so-called ministers usually don't demonstrate the power of God. No wonder they don't want you to seek His hand. They don't even know what is in His hands. I have dealt with this anti-supernaturalism of others throughout my ministry.

Later, we learned that the man Brother Osborn was ministering to had suffered a spinal injury by an explosion during the Vietnam War. His wife said that from his return home until that night in Dallas, he had not walked one step. She had been pushing him around in that wheelchair.

Then, Brother Osborn told him, *"If I were Jesus, I would say to you, 'This is your last day in a wheelchair.' If I were Jesus I would say to you, 'Your spine is healed.'"* Brother Osborn did not know about the injury in the natural, but found out afterwards. God will give you the right words to say.

God will give you words to speak over your own mind, body, family, and your children.

Brother Osborn kept talking like that, when all of a sudden, there was a stirring and the man in the wheelchair leaned forward. Osborn said, *"Jesus is here in Dallas. If I were Jesus, I would say, 'Stand-up.' I would say, 'Your legs are getting the feeling back.' Right now, God is healing your back! If I were*

Jesus, I'd tell you to walk."

The man began to walk after twenty years of being crippled. I found out a long time ago in Dallas, Texas, that if you teach and preach the Word, if you minister by the power of the Holy Spirit, if you preach that there is nothing too hard for God, then the possible comes into the realm where man has been told it is impossible and that nothing will work. God says it will work!

DEALING WITH THE SPIRIT OF INFIRMITY

Beloved, believe not every spirit, but TRY THE SPIRITS whether they are of God: because many false prophets are gone out into the world.

1 John 4:1

One of the gifts of the Spirit that aids in ministering to the oppressed is *"Discerning of Spirits" (1 Corinthians 12:10).*

I will deal with this gift in the next chapter, but it is important to note that many who are oppressed have a spirit that needs to be dealt with. In the Gospels, one out of every three people Jesus dealt with had a spirit that caused their oppression and even possession.

To be effective in the ministry to those oppressed of the devil, we need to learn how to preach in such a way that these devils are dealt with.

And he came down with them, and stood in the plain, and the company of his disciples, and a great multitude of people out of all Judæa and Jerusalem, and from the sea coast of Tyre and Sidon, which came to HEAR him, and to BE HEALED of their diseases; and they that were vexed with UNCLEAN SPIRITS: and they were healed.

Luke 6:17, 18

CHAPTER THREE
DEALING WITH DEVILS

The Spirit of the Lord is upon me, because he hath anointed me to preach the gospel to the poor; he hath sent me to heal the brokenhearted, to preach DELIVERANCE TO THE CAPTIVES, and recovering of sight to the blind, to SET AT LIBERTY THEM THAT ARE BRUISED.

Luke 4:18

Jesus' earthly ministry is recorded in the Gospel of Luke. It starts with His birth, and finishes with His resurrection. Luke also wrote the book of Acts, which connects the two books with the ascension of Christ, the birth of the Church, the apostles' ministry, and Paul's ministry.

Luke 4 records the temptation of Christ and how He dealt with the devil in the wilderness. If we are to minister to the oppressed, then we will have to deal with the devil and his demons. God has given us supernatural gifts to minister to the oppressed.

LEVELS AND DEVILS

The Apostle Paul set forth this understanding to the Ephesians:

> **For we wrestle not against flesh and blood, but against principalities, against powers, against the rulers of the darkness of this world, against spiritual wickedness in high places.**
>
> **Ephesians 6:12**

1. Principalities
2. Powers
3. Rulers of the darkness of this world
4. Spiritual wickedness in high places

The first three levels operate here on the Earth. The fourth level is wicked spirits that rule from the heavens or "high places." The Apostle Paul speaks of this fourth level of devils:

> **I knew a man in Christ above fourteen years ago, (whether in the body, I cannot tell; or whether out of the body, I cannot tell: God knoweth;) such an one caught up to the third heaven.**
>
> **2 Corinthians 12:2**

> **And lest I should be exalted above measure through the abundance of the revelations, there was given to me**

a thorn in the flesh, **THE MESSENGER OF SATAN to buffet me, lest I should be exalted above measure.**

2 Corinthians 12:7

The seventh verse reveals that Paul was that man in Christ. He was caught up into the third heaven, and a demon spirit was assigned to buffet Paul to keep him from receiving further revelations from the Lord.

We also see that there are demons that do Satan's bidding— *"The Messenger of Satan" (2 Corinthians 12:7).*

Webster's definition of *"principalities"* is given as rank or jurisdiction. I believe that the four levels listed in Ephesians 6:12 are the order of their rank.

The strong man would be the *"rulers of darkness"* *"No man can enter into a strong man's house, and spoil his goods, except he will first bind the strong man; and then he will spoil his house." (Mark 3:27)*

These spirits rule over regions. The prince of Persia that Daniel dealt with is an example. *(Daniel 10:13)*

There are spirits which cause deafness and blindness. *(Mark 9:25; Luke 7:21)*

There are unclean spirits *(Mark 3:11)*, and there are lying spirits *(2 Chronicles 18:21).*

There are spirits which cause diseases *(Luke 13:11).* There is a foul tormenting spirit of fear *(2 Timothy 1:7; 1 John 4:18).*

Every devil is subject to the power of Christ, including Satan himself *(James 2:19; Romans 14:11).*

How God anointed Jesus of Nazareth with the Holy Ghost and with power: who went about doing good, and HEALING ALL that were oppressed of the devil; for God was with him.

Acts 10:38

Oppression is the work of the devil. Acts 10:38 says sickness is an oppression of the devil.

THE IMPORTANCE OF THE DISCERNING OF SPIRITS

The great apostle Paul, the same man who was inspired to write two-thirds of the New Testament, the man that the Lord gave the revelation concerning spiritual gifts, found himself in need of the Gifts of the Spirit and in particular the discerning of spirits while he was in Philippi.

And it came to pass, as we went to prayer, a certain damsel POSSESSED WITH A SPIRIT OF DIVINA-TION met us, which brought her masters much gain by soothsaying: the same followed Paul and us, and cried, saying, These men are the servants of the most high God, which shew unto us the way of salvation. And this did she many days. But Paul, being grieved, turned and said to the spirit, I command thee in the name of Jesus Christ to come out of her. And he came out the same hour.

Acts 16:16-18

The gift of *discerning of spirits* sees into the spirit realm. It is not just devils but it encompasses the *Spirit* of God, the *spirit of man, angels,* and *demons.* As is the case in all of the operations of the Gifts of the Spirit it works at that given moment by that selfsame Spirit.

The woman followed them for many days before Paul felt in his spirit the demon. The moment that he was grieved, then he turned and dealt with the spirit of divination at that moment. The demon was referred to as *"he" (Acts 16:18),* and came out of the girl and she was free from that possession.

THE POWERFUL NAME OF JESUS

And these signs shall follow them that believe; In MY NAME shall they cast out devils; they shall speak with new tongues;

Mark 16:17

I love that Name.
I preach by that Name.
I heal the sick in that Name.
I cast out devils in that Name.
HIS NAME IS JESUS!
Deliverance is God's prescription for every soul. While I was in Atlanta, the CDC released statistics concerning the mental health of the Nation. 18 million souls are oppressed, taking antidepressants, between the ages of 18 to 40. Men

and women, boys and girls being tormented, fearful, worried and filled with anxiety.

In 2016, America was listed as the healthiest nation on the Earth; six years later, it stands at 79th. How does this happen unless there is some kind of demon power that is trying to destroy you and your family? Where are the preachers that will stand in their pulpits and declare that the devil is a liar?

Hallelujah! If everything seems against you and the numbers are against you, and if everyone is speaking against you, there is One who is for you! His Name is Jesus Christ. He is the Son of the living God. Glory to His Name!

I SAW A DEVIL POSSESS A GIRL

My wife and I were holding a meeting in a large auditorium in Canada. There was a fine young preacher in that meeting whose father and I traveled together in the early 70s. When I saw him we invited he and his wife to come back stage for fellowship. There was a table with some fruit and soft drinks. I wanted to see how they were doing.

He went over to the front row and spoke to his wife. Suddenly I saw a circle — a dark shape — right over her head. Then I saw it go right in her head and disappear into her body. When he came back I asked him where is your wife? He told me she did not want to come back. The Lord spoke to me at that moment, *"That was an unclean spirit that she opened herself up to."*

Less than a year later, his father called me. He wanted me to pray for his son and daughter-in-law. I told him *"Don't tell me anything else. Let me tell you what I saw. Your daughter in law has cheated on your son."*

"Who told you?" He asked. *"Not only that, she moved out and is living with a man and just told us she is pregnant with his child."* She ended up leaving that man and had more children by several men.

If you want to minister to the oppressed of the devil, you are going to need the power and anointing of the Holy Ghost that came in His fullness after Jesus shed His blood on the Cross. The Holy Ghost has sealed that work, and there is deliverance for every soul. There is a balm in Gilead, a healing power, a salve that when you put it upon the wounded, they shall be whole!

STEPS THAT LEAD TO DEMON POSSESSION

After the Vietnam War, I traveled extensively in Indiana from 1974 into the early '90's. While staying in Marion, I saw a minister on television teaching on deliverance from demons. His name was Lester Sumrall.

Five years later, in 1979, I found myself sitting across from the man I had seen on TV five years before. I was a young 24-year-old evangelist, and he was a veteran minister who had built great works for God around the world.

After the interview, he invited me to go over to his church on Ireland road. We went into a room with shelves filled with the different books he had written. He began to put different books in my hands. One of the books he gave me was *"Seven Ways to Recognize Demon Power Today."* Brother Sumrall told me to read them and I did. I still have all those books in my library today.

There are three avenues that the devil uses to oppress and bind people. He comes against your *body* to trouble your *mind* to possess your *spirit.* The enemy takes steps to come against you,

He uses the *spirit of infirmity* to bring sickness and disease to your body. We read in Luke 13:11, *"And, behold, there was a woman which had a spirit of infirmity eighteen years, and was bowed together, and could in no wise lift up herself."*

The devil uses the *spirit of fear* to attack the mind or soul of a person. There are a variety of emotions that the enemy uses to oppress and depress a mind. Most mental conditions are birthed from fear. We are encouraged that, *"For God hath not given us the spirit of fear; but of power, and of love, and of a sound mind." (2 Timothy 1:7)*

Then there is the *spirit of antichrist.*

And every spirit that confesseth not that Jesus Christ is come in the flesh is not of God: and this is that spirit of antichrist, whereof ye have heard that it should come; and even now already is it in the world.

1 John 4:3

I heard a minister say that sometimes when you sense heaviness in your spirit it is because your righteousness is rubbing up against the world's unrighteousness. Remember, *"Greater is he that is in you, than he that is in the world. (1 John 4:4)*

The enemy works from the outside in. The Holy Spirit works from the inside to the out. A Christian cannot be demon possessed.

There are certainly steps that can bring on destruction to men and women. Our heart as believers should be to help the helpless and heal the hurting.

Judas took steps because of his pride and greed that led him to suicide. Demas walked away from the anointing. *"For Demas hath forsaken me, having loved this present world, and is departed unto Thessalonica;" (2 Timothy 4:10)*

However, it is God's will that every soul be free. *"The Lord is not slack concerning his promise, as some men count slackness; but is longsuffering to us-ward, NOT WILLING THAT ANY SHOULD PERISH , but that all should come to repentance." (2 Peter 3:9)*

DELIVER ME

When a man or woman takes steps away from the Word of God then they are wide open for the devil to lead them to destruction by the work of seducing spirits and doctrines of devils. *(1 Timothy 4:1)*

Our battle is not just with the devil but demonic forces, but there is victory in Jesus! There was a time in King David's life that he cried out to God, *"DELIVER ME from bloodguiltiness, O God, thou God of my salvation: and my tongue shall sing aloud of thy righteousness." (Psalm 51:14)*

Over the years, I have discovered that the devil uses many means to destroy people. Loneliness, discouragement, sorrow, grief, stress, mental worry, anxiety, financial lack, sickness and disease . . . troubles!

The day came when David cried out to God and his prayer is the pathway for our deliverance.

CREATE in me a clean heart, O God; and RENEW a right spirit within me. Cast me not away from thy presence; and take not thy holy spirit from me. RESTORE unto me the joy of thy salvation; and uphold me with thy free spirit.

Psalm 51:10-12

My prayer is that you will get free and stay free in Jesus' Name!

DOWNLOAD OUR APP.

Search "Ted Shuttlesworth" in the Apple App Store or the Google Play Store.

DO YOU NEED PRAYER?

Call us today: 1-888-323-2484

Visit us online: www.tedshuttlesworth.com